Soon

Soon

Fait Muedini

K&B

Published by:

Kennedy & Boyd,
an imprint of
Zeticula Ltd,
Unit 13,
44-46 Morningside Road,
Edinburgh, EH10 4BF
Scotland

http://www.kennedyandboyd.co.uk

First published in 2025

Text © Fait Muedini 2025

Rubáiyát of Omar Khayyám, translated by Edward
Fitzgerald, stanza lxiii, 3rd edition, 1872

Cover image © francescoch 2025

ISBN 978-1-84921-259-5 paperback

Acknowledgements

I want to thank Kaltrina, Edon, Dua, Atli and Mudzefer Muedini.

vi

Contents

"Oh threats of Hell and Hopes of Paradise!
One thing at least is certain — *This* Life flies,
    One thing is certain and the rest is Lies;
The Flower that once has blown for ever dies."

--Rubáiyát of Omar Khayyám

Resist by Renaissance

A laundry list of longing.

Burn sage secluded in an isolated, self-selected sanctuary.
        The road outside awaits.

Systematic, symbiotic syllables
travel through tumultuous terrains.

Observe the extravagance.
        The fireworks of fortune
                are just outside your balcony window.

Widows wonder whether
life laughs lightly, or cries,
cackles or offers empathetic condolences
        for what transpired.

The universe is not a shoulder to cry on. The universe is here to
ultimately take you away.

Time taunts.

Resist by renaissance. Every breath is a rebellion against the
rationality of work.

Mundane social constructs, and everyone miserable themselves
        look to dig your grave
                        with their own regrets.

Tomorrow, Eventually, There Will Be No Tomorrow

Whirl madly.

Trinkets of gold tempt.
         Pay no mind.
Instead,
         wade the waters
                                        unhabituated
         studying smiles of the seductress.

None of this will not happen again.

So, pick dandelions aimlessly
         or skydive off mountains recklessly.

You are but a tourist.

Mountains of wealth won't change the fact that
you are getting older.

Why oscillate between the coastlines of "should I" and "shouldn't
I"?

Wealth lies in the coffers of s/he who empties those very same
coffers for
the wars of love.

Let ambition marry aspiration.

Tomorrow, eventually, there will be no tomorrow.

The Recognition That Everything Melts Away

The drippings of deceased snowflakes
    serve as the clearest form of evidence
        that death is never but an arm's distance.
    Here today
        but gone the moment their body hits the ground.

This is but an introspective glance into the reality
    that the elements of a long life are but an illusion.
The world will come for you
    much like the way these little magnificent floating
masterpieces
meet their demise.

What makes you any more special than these
    illustrious, crystalized paintings?

Our time on Earth feels as short as their lifespan.

    Understand this now,
        or learn this painful lesson later.

Children want to capture these fluttering figures of form
    with the hopes of keeping them forever
only to
    ultimately realize
        that everything
            melts
        away.

Thieves

At the end of it all,
    will you look back and wonder,
        (while never forgiving yourself)
            as to how you let ruthless thieves
                enter your mind
and steal such precious time.

Dreams Departing on Dusty Streets

Dreams departing on dusty streets.
    A small suitcase and a signed letter
        sealed and stuffed in the back pocket.

Someday, when old, drunk, and angry,
    the sound of sadness
        will ring incessantly in your ear.

This shall be a day of reckoning.

    Everything that needs to be said has already been written.
        The soul already knowns what sins have been
committed

    and what dreams were let to
    walk away.

Like a desperate lover, dash out and plead
    for just one more chance.

See, dreams are forgiving. They understand that life is
complicated,
    and that the mind is
        fickle in its desires, and easily distracted and
    disheveled.
    So, they prefer to grant clemency.

But play around enough
    toying with the word "tomorrow" so many times
        that at some point
the woman who waited patiently for a ring of commitment
    will tolerate no more.

    You will eventually become a shell of yourself
        at the tail end of life
opening a letter from an identity past
    one who had a clear vision for the dreams destined
        yet squandered everything
who now sits back and wonders,

    "Where did it all go?"

Without Any Hint

I caught myself committing sin,
      for I offered a heavy sigh,
frustrated with the momentary lot in life
      after I stepped outside in the pouring rain
            becoming drenched under dreary skies.

But then, just as quickly, I recanted
            and begged for forgiveness.

But time heard
      and simply smiled.

We both understood each other.

      I took for granted what shall eventually become out of my
grasp.

There will be many, many more downpours
      outside of my consciousness,
            outside of myself.

The universe shall continue to buzz along
      without any hint of me.

Yet somehow, I had the audacity to become bothered with
      the ecstatic experience of existence.

It is Here that You Were Meant to Grace the Cosmos

How many summers are prescribed?

From this number, subtract the years where your body will be long
past its prime,
   for the ancient and the new are not one.

The question thus becomes,
   "What will you do with this forecast,
     this prophecy
         this omen?"

The slow, subdued state of servitude to Father Time
   severs all security and shocks all sense of the endless self.

So, speak the language of being fully alive.

Hit those waves harder.
Immerse yourself into the abyss of absoluteness.
Whatever you feel lights the fire of desire,
   where passion permeates,
     make that your temple.

It is here that you were meant to grace the cosmos.

A Fateful Severance

Look at the moon's glow tonight
    its radiance
        its history
           its pain
    and understand
        that sooner or later
           you won't see another.

A fateful severance.

The Assembly of the Awestruck

Five hundred years from now,
     time ventures out and buys a sledgehammer
        to smash your sepulcher
           ensuring any evocations
              and prayers over the pir are
        obliterated.
Obsolete; a sojourn overextended.

     Since your momentous farewell, Earth has turned its
back.

Thousands of circumventions

     and you are no longer present for any of them.
Know this now.

Aware and advised,
     appropriate energy
        and join the Assembly of the Awestruck.
They who place their piercing eyes at the absolute astonishment
of the everything.

The beauty beholden in an unfiltered trance of tranquility.

An adoration seen in an entirety of an emphatic observation.
     An overcoming of indescribable joy.

This is a life unbounded.
     This is a life unguarded.
We live gracefully accepting the bounties of what has been
bequeathed
     but for a short time.

With This, We Have in Our Hands All Possibilities

Starve the voice of reason when you are the attorney for the heart.
Proclaim the crime of passion from mountaintops
and from dripping wet rainfalls on unexpected
summer nights.

What is to remain of lost opportunities
that were stinted because
paradise was waiting at its door
for the wanderer who, on this day, decided not to show?

I tell extravagant tales after burying regrets in deep ditches, in
deserted deserts.

Omar Khayyam is asleep, but his words sing through the voice of
the muezzin
who
on that day,
forgot the words of the Quran
and instead,
remembered to cease all learnedness
and just be.

With this, we have in our hands all possibilities.

Nietzsche's Call to Prayer

Pity those sad souls who misinterpret soon
      for soon enough.

As if God will
      suddenly change the laws of nature
            to grant you the privilege to see all that could
have be seen.
This was the sole purpose of life,
      but
            "little do you take heed."

What sadness,
      to watch the so called 'spiritual'
            stepping over the sacred
                  in searching for the very same
sacred.
Waiting for death
      in order to live.

Those who ignore Nietzsche's call to prayer deserve absolutely
nothing.

In dying,
      the comprehension that what was perfect
          was perfectly positioned,
             but taken completely for granted.

Be Not the Gullible Guest

Ample potentialities
        rest softly in your heart and in your soul.
The morning has greeted you:
        "Welcome Back."

But it's a cold, cold host.
        The day shall shower you with delicious croissants
                the very same ones sprinkled with powdered
sugar
                        and topped with sliced almonds
                                and chocolate. Lots and lots of
chocolate.
You will never want to leave.
        But then, just as you get comfortable,
                beginning to lay your legs onto plush couches,
                        thinking that you could live like this
forever,
BAM!
        Time kicks you out of its home forever.

So, be not a gullible guest in thinking that you are the exception.

Because of this,
        know what is around the corner,
                while still being bewildered with the banquets of
        breakfast.

        Sample fine cheeses,
                the aged blues, and the White Stilton
Gold,
                      and so, so much more.
      And dance,
                dance to the music
                uninhibited.
Be unequivocally in love with the *this*,

so much so that every moment is a grinding of
teeth in passion.

The pure expression of both joy
and that pain the comes with the pressure.

But understand this well:

she shall leave you just enough time,
to make a few phone calls,
to gather your belongings,
to prepare yourself for
departure.

Meanwhile,

time will throw another party,
another celebration,
with another fool who,
invited,
naively thinks that he is the man of the
hour
and that the festivities shall go
on forever.
Little does he know,
that the gala was never really meant for him.

Therefore,
sit here with certainty,
relishing every minute
of being the temporary traveler,
who just so happens to have been invited to lodge lavishly.

Know that you will soon wear out your welcome.

But before then, cause chaos in celebration.
The door is wide open,
until it isn't.

Forever Again Unreachable

I stretch my arms
    not unlike a newborn

        who has, for the first time,
           entered the world,
             a wonder.
Let this be the ritual for each morning.
      Yesterday's images were yesterday's images.
      Tomorrow, we have yet to receive any such gifts.
      Today, what the eyes see are sacred in and of
        themselves.
A first encounter.
      Sure, you may have seen the sun before.

      But that was before.

Here, we witness again,
    observation afresh.
Understand that each dynamic rests on the lack of longevity.
    Soon, what is experienced
        shall wither and die.
The beauty is beholden to the temporary.

Travel with this mindset.
    The crowds will crow and call you crazy.
      Pay them absolutely no mind.
If mystics are not mystified at the ever-present beauty of the now,
    then when will they ever become amazed by anything?
God is here,
    staring straight into your soul
urging you to partake in the phenomenon that is *this*.

Wish for wonder and youth all you want.
      But remember that the gifts gracing us today
        shall depart for a journey

forever again

      unreachable.

For the Greater Good That is Your Life

Circle back to the day before the departure
        the morning when the bread crunched upon
biting,
                when the leaf wrapped cheese captured the
Rogue River within its midst
                        and the taste was nothing short of an
unrivaled sense of fervor.

Senile seniors who squandered years
        sit on park benches
uttering to whomever will listen
        to attend the concerts of songbirds
who sing stories about heartache, about ardor,
        about instances that suspend the notion of time.

Not understanding a verbal language is no excuse for
not leading with your emotions:
                                smiles are universal.

Bid adieu
        to your childhood home,
        to your youth,
        to your beloved,
        to your everything.

        Saying those words will happen whether you are ready or
not.

        Write your *maranasati* on your mirror each morning.

The objective is to ensure your memories are plentiful, and that
they hold your older self not in the shackles of regret for
        restricting all the majesty that could have been.

Caramel covered cupcakes sit proudly in quaint pastry shops
        lined together as organized soldiers,
                all except one, who just had to be sacrificed
        separately for the greater good
that is your life.

Let Death Deal with Its Jealousy

Faint fog hangs over city skies.
Small shop owners starting to turn keys and signs.
Open for business.
Another day of potential.

Steaming coffee machines
long pastries laid out one after the other;
resembling railway tracks to the
tastebuds,
and caskets to the morbid.

Revel in the revival of the morning.
Another evening, conquered.

See yourself smile in the Earth's resistance.
See yourself shine in the signs of subsistence.

Today, let death deal with its jealousy.
For you are alive and free,
and it, bitter and disgruntled at the fact that
you have yet to fall.

But trust me.
This cold-hearted killer is looking for an angle,
any angle,
to end you.
But until its grip squeezes your soul,
know this:
this entity is absolutely helpless.

Rejoice in this realization.
Death hates you living
as much as you hate dying.

So live.
If not out of an urgency,
or even an appreciation of all that the universe
offers,
if nothing else,
live out of spite.

Awake from a slumber
so revealing, so penetrable, so deep.

The world was meant to be seen with seductive
eyes.

Landscapes sit beaming with life.

So, what are you waiting for?

Tomorrow never announces why it eventually decides to
stop showing up.
But when nonappearance occurs,
you will be left with a mountain of
regret.

Face the winds head on.

Start small.
Visit the local ice cream shop
the very same building
you have driven by countless times.
Sit and sip a strawberry milkshake
and savor the soundless mornings of a cold January
winter.

From here, find the local nature preserve.
Lace up the tough hiking boots
and become absorbed in the field entirely.

Over time, while crossing off item after item
a transformation takes place.

A taunting of tomorrow, even.
Why? Because in the experiences grows
a new being
one who is not only more versed in the *now*,
but also,
one who is no longer afraid of death.

Utter "Do to me what you will,"
and then laugh.

Sinister? Not in the slightest.

All that is being witnessed
is the soul who has escaped the echo chamber
of societal expectations of existence.

At this station: everything else is but a bonus.
The world, these stars, the crisp ground on a frigid
morning.
All of it. The entirety.
Much appreciated extensions of the
space
that we call life.

The Lesson of the Rose

Learn from the petals of the rose.
      They blushed beautifully
red revealed throughout
        stems standing tall
           flaunting florescence.
               They spoke when it was their time to
    speak.

But we cry for the bare bud.

What is no more is no more.

Are you somehow the exception?

    Think not for an instance lest you lie to yourself.

We mourn the magnificence of a flower so revered.
      One, when birthed, blossomed.
         Yet, a reminder that what remains today
           is but a withered weed.

Our fate is close.
      Take this tale and embrace your existence
         by bleeding the genuineness of your attributes
         vividly and vibrantly.

The rose may have expired, but centuries later
      the opulence of its authentic aura continues
unquestioned.

With Innocent Eyes

With innocent eyes
    detached from a dream, so extravagant.
        sitting with solemn vows scribbled
            onto fallen leaves
        yet to turn crisp
            with another cold winter approaching.

Wedding bells ring for someone.
        The one attached shall eventually become jilted.
        Here, heartache follows a heartbreak.

        Premonitions of
            Sunday morning strolls down
                dormant boulevards.

Hand holding and verse sharing
    secrets abound.
        Sooner or later, someone is sure to acquiesce.

Captivated by far-from-common characters, lined with specialty
next to one another,
        forming words that somehow have the capacity
            to light a soul on fire.

Wonder not how this is possible.
    Tomorrow is not here for interpretation.

        A future self is sure to steer the mind back to this
moment.

Today, diagnose not
    how you reached this point
        of staring at the darling
            whose words blurred the lines between
being and non-being
salvation and accursed,
    unbounded prospectives

and a surreal solo death.
The mind has a habit of building hills of interpretation to
    narratives naïve in nature.

This is no time to decipher.
        So instead,
                stare in awareness
                        and recognize the abundance
                            of this perfect present.
Do so with innocent eyes.

We Have These Days

We have these days
        until we no longer have these days.

Tomorrow is the Cessation of Time

Tomorrow is the cessation of time
        for some tortured soul

who
        with a wish list and a pocket finally full of cash
                    (so carefully collected from decades of
                    soul-sucking work)
just.ran.out.of.time.

You somehow think none of this applies.

They thought the same.
They always think the same.

The Timepiece

Say your goodbyes to yesterday
    by not saying goodbye.

Stepping away needs no introduction nor conclusion.

Clouds are clouds because they are clouds.

Living in your mind means
    not living in the present.

Who wants to waste what wonderful minutes remain
    coiled in the watch springs?
When the movement runs out,
    there shall be no ability to rewind.

The timepiece shall merely sit in some glamorous box
    put far away,
never again to see the light of day.

The Golden Crown

An early morning fascination with
        frost on automobile windows.

One of but a trillion miracles.

The world is nothing but a breathtaking beauty
        and you have been granted full permission to stare
                ...for as long as your life allows, that is.
So take the opportunity and
        fall in love, in perpetuity.

The move to the cold, hardened box always awaits.

Observe, observe, and observe. Write with an unwavering intent.
        Smell fragrances sent from lands afar
                mixed in labs
                        and sprayed on soft skins, with
subtleness.

Cherish wandering down a grocery isle,
        where fruits are plentiful and profound
                where cakes are perfectly placed
                        eye level and inescapable to experience,
                                at least but a slice.
This world is our playground.
        Eventually, an ever so soon eventually of
                what were once thoughts of the limitless options
                        become a war of attrition
                                to just stay alive.
Our time is best be served living like kings.

        Then, when cornered and captured
                at least we leave this world
                        having worn the golden crown.

The Final Concert

Take in the violin's state of mourning
while sitting still by the windowsill.

      Open air and an aroma of affection.
An aura of invisibility
      as the notes permeate with providence.
A provenance unlike no other.
      A beauty unlike no other.

Quiet captivation
      as the musician plays the last concert of her life.

Here you are to witness the mystery of play
          the festering of emotions finally
     resolved.

      Throw flowers before throwing flowers.
        Afterwards, take yourself completely out of the
picture.

             The
             universe is
             greater than all
             its parts.
Do nothing but observe.
Do nothing but cry expressions of bliss.

The Ever-Declining Number of Tomorrows

The unexplored desires
      that are dressed up in an immaculate language of goals
         are unfortunately often left ever so loosely to
languish in a deserted dresser drawer.

These will be the markers of regret
      upon the eyes and heart of a frail, frail old man.

Who is arrogant enough to not understand
      that we will not witness the world
         for much longer?
Everything pushes us towards the cliff of non-existence.

And yet, you still scribble desires in notebooks?

      Tear out those pages and staple them to the door of the
mosque.

This is happening, and it's happening now.

The conviction of living out life
      must be our only religion.

The stars are out in full force
      almost taunting you to travel
and yet somehow, you say the word "someday?"

Senile and sorrowful. There is no other way to describe
      the sad soul who seems to bet the farm on 'forever
tomorrow' when
the tomorrows are continuously lessening in number.

The Demon of Demons

The demon of demons runs through the libraries of the world
      closing each and every open book.
This unstoppable force laughs as it sees humankind hold onto the
ideas of knowledge
      and the accumulation of things.

Tomorrow turns its back on everyone.

Space for writing narratives and telling tales shall become extinct,
      and amphitheaters will sit empty on account of audiences
that cease to exist.

Therefore, what use is fretting about how actions are perceived?

What a wasteful undertaking.

The oceans are calling you to swim this evening,
      and music,
for you to dance.

Anything else,
      outside the scope of love,
            is nothing but nonsense.

Sublime Time

True sympathies are
   somehow tangled and twisted
in a complex roadmap of wishes and wants.

You may have thought death would surely have visited a decade or
two ago.

Thus remember
   for the rest of your life
      that you dodged a bullet.

So yes, living on extended time.
   Living on sublime time.

Staring in Serenity

The melting of minds.
A special realization.
A cognition of majestic proportions.

Staring in serenity
        speaking in speechless tongues.

We are here now, and we are not here soon.
        This is enough to cover any canvas with paint.

Splurge,
        and love.

Write poetic letters.
        Linger in each other's presence
                for as long as the sun keeps quiet.

In the morning, a doleful absence of celestial carnations.

Since That Many Decades Ago

We all await the announcement of death delivered.

      At some point
one cannot help but reflect on just
        how far back this anticipation has gone.

      Midday mischief
kicking soccer balls into heavy guarded gardens
        and climbing up and down a split level.
           Having fallen once,
the subdued Saturday,
      or Sunday,
           or Monday...
How—with ever so much assurance—
        time has indeed blown its presence through our hair
           since that many decades ago.

Must Move on and Live

Who counts the number of times death could come
        before even stepping out each day and at least trying this
thing called life?

How have you allowed negativity to so easily creep into the garden
and strangle
        all healthy flowers?

Today is a gateway to just how cheerfully you will smile on your
deathbed,
        where, if approached well,
                there are neither "thank-yous" nor apologies,
                        with gratitude being but the glorious
gaze.

Never let events like funerals fall in the way of wandering,
wondering, witnessing.
        Respect and remember.
                But then shortly after, surely, you must move on
and live.

Mirrors of Exuberance

Every walk to the waterfall is a rejuvenation of attitude
        a gratefulness in observation that within the current
                lies the awareness of life, vibrating,
fostering images of breath, of color, of revelation
        in flower petals, in trees shading nearby, in smiles of a
youth yet departed.

In age, grace
        and piles of dusty books
a room filled with clutter
        yet, hesitant to throw out what ultimately will be
cleared by the next scholar.

        The thralls of thinking.

Fear of forgetting is what drives accumulation.
        Time has already swept away files without asking for
approval.

Quiet walks, quintessential curiosity and a bevy of brewed coffee
cups.

In everything, mirrors of clarity.
In everything, mirrors of exuberance.

Marble Teeth

The memory and forgetfulness of generations that
    we
          with certainty
tie ourselves to homelands
      with the belief that the barons of these grounds will live
forever.
Oh, how so wrong we are.

The same paved roads will lay witness to new births
      and other eventual deaths.

The mountains have no time to lament.

    Take but a few steps
        and then depart, for the burial fields
            become ever more matriculated,
              only with ever fewer
family members to identify the demarcations.

Eventually, the entire graveyard smiles
      showing its marble teeth
    within a world that won't eventually harbor
a single soul as witness
    to testify that
        "Yes, these lives were lived."

Lived While Alive

I wander aimlessly
      without intent
            wistfully ignorant of the word
                tomorrow.

Instilled in the insulated love of the now,
      nothing else makes sense.

I don't ever look back at muddy tracks left behind.
      What is behind, is behind, is behind.

Manna cannot be tasted in the yesterday.
      Storing succulent sweets quenches not the craving of he
          who is scheduled to be hung at dawn.
Shine all sunlight on my head
      the saintly halo in all paintings.

Alive. The description of the mystic who pushes aside all outside
the present.
      Why do people waste time writing long epitaphs on
tombstones?

               Here lies (*You*)_____
               Lived while Alive.

Craft Experiences That Will Be Fodder for Future Deathbed Recollections

Forty years ago
Your mother held you gently
rocked you to sleep
and must have wondered,

just "Wow."

Today, decades later,
passing by multiple moonlights
and vast lands sprawled
        with memories racing after memories.

What was once an eternity at youth is now ever closer to ending.

We sit staring at stars
        and giving thanks for the operability of our ability to be
attune with
the glories of the galaxy.

I atone for nothing, and wade my feet in warm waters
        sensing the serenity of everything in and around me.

Time is ticking.
        We extrapolate the inevitable and adjust life accordingly.
So sad: youth shackled by the judgements of society. Quickly will
your age, age.
Seemingly momentarily all that was dreamed for
becomes all that is lost.
        Until change is impossible, change is possible.
An empty duffle bag is waiting for a change of scenery,
        asking to be stuffed in an overhead compartment, or
thrown in the back of some
                spacious trunk.

Let the now be your normal.
Life sprung decades ago,
    and is sure to cease in decades to come.

But now,
        now,
                craft experiences that will be fodder for future
deathbed recollections.

Neglected Sunsets

No sensations survive
    and so,
        all ignorance ends tonight.

Have you no faith in yourself?

You have lost thirst for the final few days left
    on Earth?

What is the matter?

    --Soon, all will be gone--

~~Repeat this mantra~~
Repeat this death sentence.
    Ensure that the words are seared clear into your mind,
without escape, without excuse.

    A life ever loosening from your grasp.
One neglected sunset after another.

Here Is Your Destiny

Gurus touting reverse aging,
       while face-injected drones
drone on and on and on about staying young
       all the while looking into a mirror
and being horrified with what they see,
       what watches them back.
       That which is reflecting is not what is true
to a mind that has believed an entirely different narrative
       for the first few chapters of life.
So sorry to have the fairytale crash into a reckless sea of denial
       while you stay solo,
swimming in a sea of ever increased irrelevance.

Imagine running backwards
       through a luxury lined store,
accepting anything that was freely gifted in youth,
       but what now is outside your reach.

Not once has time shown sympathy to the aged.

Here is your destiny. Rest assured.

Extinguished

A set of assumptions
        shattered with the opening of sleepy eyes
                on this cold, cold autumn morning.

Today, the heart awakes to a reckoning
        searching frantically for time, but
lost.
        Where did the days go?
What was once an unlimited, free flowing book of pages
        gleaming in their possibilities
is now
        nothing.

The death of the flame of ambition,
        of hope,
                of possibility.

This is the old flame that the aged soul laments.
        On a deathbed covered in rose-petals,
                we glance back at life
                      and gain a glaring warmth
reflecting on the early undertakings of witnessing
        where the act and actor were indistinguishable from one
another
where the colors of the universe just merged so seamlessly together.

Those days are now long gone.

The old flame is flickering no more.

Nameless

Leave worries aside
      withering in their ever-weakening decomposition.
We recognize not an ounce of their power.

Today, tonight, tomorrow,

      the tables must be filled with spreads so extravagant
that the taste buds demand respite from such glory.

And if poverty has befallen
      and mere morsels are all that can cover the tattered
blanket,
rejoice in owning the power of being in capacity and
                in vicinity
of the ever present *now*.

At some allotted time,
      both beggar and sultan shall be less than footnotes
          and new iterations will run to revitalize the same
stresses
that the ever so few
      successfully viewed as folly.

These winds will take everyone and everything.

So,
      allow voices to carry through the household
          spilling out onto wet streets,
singing so saturated with the love of living.

Remember,
      the very same corridors
will be all that is left,
      sitting alone, witnessing silence
          where the voices of vibrant vibrations
are empty,
          long ago rendered nameless.

Eventually

The haunting voice of a beloved
> no more.

This is the gift that life gives.

So, prepare for the day of separation.

How?
> The same way Sufis face finality,
>> and the infinite nature
of

> All.

By kissing your spouse,
> and in your mind,
>> uttering the phrase
>>> sung in the ear of a newborn.

"From God we came, and to God we shall return."

Spend the remaining evening cuddling with your beloved,
> watching a film,
>> all the while knowing
>>> that eventually...
>>>> eventually.

Departures

Come,
> climb this rigid branch.
>> Peer upon the clouds above
>>> and the grasslands below.

Be beseeched with new beginnings.

The hostile nature of nature loves to slam the book at various
points of the story.
> A surprise ending before the surprise ending.

And somehow,
> we think that when the master storyteller tells our tale
>> that somehow
> we shall be treated differently.

What a sad, sad lie we tell ourselves.

The world is indifferent.

Therefore
> use that emptiness and witness with fresh eyes.

Tomorrow is a tomorrow that cannot be rewound,
> nor a story rewritten.

The gleaming sensation of earth shining in its eminence
> seeing itself
> dancing alone
> dying defiantly.

The utter illuminations of an existence both devoid of
> and deep in
>> detailed departures.

Death, in One Manifestation or Another, Lurks

Fall in love with the world
    one breath at a time.

Be incapable of hiding the heat you feel.

      Every single morning the sun stretches out
                        an aura of
                        calmness.
      This is the witnessing of those with luxury eyes.

They who have taken painstaking efforts to refine their
perceptions
      now taste the riches of their dedication.

An army of observers meditate on rigid shorelines
      some in lotus, others lounging, and a few walking

wanderers.
 A single stroke of nature's pen
                        can wipe out all
wherewithal,
         all excitement,
            all instances of peace.

The day is marked with invisible ink.
    Know this.

      Never forget that there is a bounty on your head
          and in due time, the order will be carried out
with sharp precision.
Death, in one manifestation or another, lurks.

Death Shall Have the Last Laugh

Oh well rested ones,
  the day is now clearly in front of your face.

    Fully charged,
      so charge forward.

Flee the thoughts of resistance
  be they logistics,
      the condition of the abode upon your departure
  or society's judging eyes.

Everything will work itself out.

Check off another sunrise from the calendar of your life.
  No more than the allotted ever gets added. Ever.

Therefore, throw confetti for no particular reason.

      the justification for doing anything
is knowing,
    quite well,
        that in no time,
            there will be no time.

Meditate on that.
Dwell on that.
Die on that.

Cities and countrysides are teeming with potentialities
    and you, with your pre-death to do list,
        lazily avoid any semblance of urgency.
Death shall have the last laugh.
    Death always has the last laugh.

Borrowed Time

Count your blessings the same way
    a thief counts gold coins,
with gratitude, for pulling off the heist of a lifetime.

    How are you here? How are you *still* here?
    A fulfilled wonderment.

Looking over your shoulder, awaiting death to nab you,
    almost as if to say, "You didn't think it would be that easy,
did you?"

But to your bewilderment, the reaper is nowhere to be found.

Soon,
    the robber begins to take their work for granted,
        becoming ever more so complacent,
            leaving fingerprints,
    and in the case of life,
        by uttering a single word:
tomorrow.

I am healthy, I am free, I have wealth, so, tomorrow...
    tomorrow.

No one ever anticipates an apprehension by authorities.
    No one ever expects that fated tap on the shoulder.

But know this:
    eventually, you will be taken down.

A demise of the mortal is anticipated.

So, take the gift of freedom today and live with the understanding
    that the entirety of life is nothing but borrowed time.

Birthday Morning

Today,
          a gloomy reminder that
                    the last dance
is closer than ever before.

This has always been the case
          and will always stay the case.
However,
          on the day of birth
man takes more time
          to look back
retracing our steps
          seeing who has fallen off the journey
no longer with us
          with the recognition
that at some point
          we too shall depart from the stage.

The mind goes to memories of childhood
          blowing out candles
and receiving special video game gifts.

Once immune from time,
          this evil foe
                    becomes seemingly more deadly
with each passing year.

The monster has horns. We see them vividly
          while staring at ourselves
on a very early
          birthday morning.

The Color of the Roses on My Tombstone

Control is a creation that confiscated creativity.
    Be yourself and exude the essence of originality.

Moonlight drives through foggy farmland roads
    sip after sip after sip
        deep breath after deep breath
            one sunset stacked upon the other.
Revive lifeless bodies.
    Resuscitate with majestic music, a quick-witted poem
        or merely a smile
            which shall be
remembered forever
tattooed in the mind
    spiraling out of society

slow reverb, chopped and screwed soundtracks
    the revelation of the prophet who has mere months to
live.

        Taken seriously, and followed religiously,
preparing for death
        with dignity.

Be in constant communication with the wonder of the morning,
    the sensation of evenings
        the death of sleep,
the revitalization of dawn.

I presume that the color of the roses on my tombstone
    will be bright red.

Beaming by Being, Now

A mischievous greeting grin
      quickly tempered by a more-mild mannered, stoic stare.

The world has both failed--and also lived up to expectations.

Do with that what you will.

Record history with calligraphy that suits your story
      because life is exactly that.
Fostered feelings
      harbored wholly
an entirety of the past
      on ever so tired shoulders.
Gleam a glimpse of what (potentially) lies ahead.
      There are afternoons to waste wonderfully
            sitting on silent rockers, staring off at a pond
pondering the impermanency of life, yet the longevity of
living.
      Deceased, eventually,

but beaming by being,
      now.

Avoid

The best person to speak with
    who will
        quicker than anyone else
            jolt you into being awake during life
        is the one who is dead.
Walking, but deceased.
        Have a conversation with them
about, well, anything.
        Notice the dejection.
The monotone voice
    and the almost robotic movements.
With them, the juice has been drained
    and all that is left is a shell of self,
and even there,
    the exterior shows dejection.

Avoid this fate at all costs,
            even if this means giving up most material items
                    for the rest of
                    your earmarked days.
So be it.

        This is the price to pay
            to bypass living in a slumber
                    until the Final Slumber
where no amount of change or sacrifice
            will suffice to alter the fate the universe
has
decided for you.

As They Will Ever Be

The travesty of life is living in a sea of opinions,
      each their own strong current.

Become free and swim without wishing,
      without being weighed by unwarranted criticism.

Few will have any interest for you
      after throwing a handful of dirt onto your grave.

So, why waste any semblance of your senses on such silliness?

The possibilities of euphoria are as alive for you
      as they will ever be.

An Obituary for the Man Who Lived in Perpetual Wonder

Let the trumpeters play valiantly
    as they lay your lifeless body into the frigid tomb.

Gone, but a rebel at heart,
    a rebel in action.

Stories are told of the man who lived gallantly
    who refused to concede
        and moved with an urgency
unappreciated by outsiders.

    A million words poured from the pen
but only because a million notes were heard with
        eager ears
grateful for the glory of song.

    Eyes, hungry for images sculpted, splashed, and stained.
He wanted them all.

    Terrains traveled
        stories shared within inner abodes
sensations registered
    winds against the skin
        and pounds of different perfumes
permeated.

Intoxicating incense; cardamon; patchouli; vetiver.
    Aromas abound.

    Luscious fruits, each bite, amazing in taste.
And sweets. Scouring stores for examples of confections worth
confessing
    one's admiration for.
He ate them all.

With each bite, teardrops. Tears for beauty, and tears for time,
                    that eventually tore him apart from all this.
But not before
       an outpouring of vigorous purpose of self. An outpouring of an authentic addict for the world and its contents.

An obituary for the man who lived in perpetual wonder.

An Existence Ever So Certain, Yet Ever So Short

Oh, delicate soul,
        you shall be survived by
           name only.
But your sense of semblance,
               gone for good,
with sins and successes,
        both forever buried away from public consciousness.

The world's recollection of you
        is as deep as a small puddle on
           a quick summer rain shower.
All rain
       quickly evaporates
           and children rush out to play again,
out of mind
       as if the storm never even happened.

A sigh of relief.

      Save the spiel
          for a supposed plan of what must be.

Everyone telling you anything
      about how to live
         is attempting to take the only "you" that is real.

Towers of clocks remind us
      of what is ever so near.

Hear the faint echoes of ancestors
      offering warning and
        urging urgency.

Step not lightly on this Earth.

      And most certainly,
        don't do it wearing anyone else's shoes.

The stars have aligned for an existence ever so certain
      yet ever so short.

Freedom at its Finest

Be absolutely out of your mind.
This is the only way to dance with God.

Dismiss judges who have something to critique about your steps.

    The sunset holds no harsh words.

Raindrops will eventually hit your tombstone
      on some cold,

            secluded evening.

But tonight,

Be in control of the narrative.

Soaking wet
under the same downpour.

Only this time,
the resistance is beautiful.

Freedom at its finest.

The Emptiness That Follows Laughter

Look quite scrupulously.

Rooms of laughter
 shall eventually turn empty, quiet and cold.

 An outcome guaranteed.

The Lamp Lighting the Remainder of Life

The lamp lighting opportunity and experience
        only has oil for an appointed time.

Then afterwards,
        but a paperweight on the desk of a poet
                who resides no more in unity, or in witnessing, or
        in breathing.

The opportunity for everything is now,
        but is always ever-fleeting.

Antique flea markets are graveyards
        filled with the relics of those who once were.

That Nothing is Actually Yours

The objects we will never see again
are ever increasing.

The more we age, and the more we experience
the more entities we have to say goodbye to.

Everything is reminding you
that nothing is actually yours.

These Seconds are Swift in their Escape

Those who pass by will populate the calendar
        scheduling showings and other obligations
           all on your behalf.

Resist if necessary.

Each chore undesired by the heart
is a heavy weight on the fragility of today.

These seconds are swift in their escape.

Hours spent grieving the irreversible

                      never seem to
                find their way
                    back home.

Pick Tea

Pick tea with your parents,
      and do so quickly.

Because, before you know it,
      nothing will be around,
            neither you, nor the chai plants, nor them.

Nothing except Lake Prespa and the setting sun,
      who both laid witness to this particularly extraordinary early evening
            that once was.

Next Time

Use the phrase "next time" sporadically and with caution,
      knowing that even then,
            the most meticulous of plans
            can come undone.

Not a soul knows their last look at the moon.

      Simple conversations at a café table will eventually
become
            the final conversation while together at a café
      table.

Expectations of future encounters should be heavily discounted.

Every congregation is the lighting of a candle for the holy.

Engage with a loving veracity
      for tomorrow,
            the winds shall blow out all roaring flames.

The Condition of Cemeteries

Conversations about the condition of cemeteries.

Death is death is death.

Whether basking in the summer sun,
        or shaded under a pine tree seeping sap as its needles cast
a shadow over your grave,

all roads lead to a unified fate.

Graveyard Views

Even the very best views of Pelister are worthless
when wrapped within your grave.

The time for hiking and witnessing is now.

It will always be now.

Celebrate the process of living,
       so death cannot take even an ounce of you.

Be vigilant in vibrant experiencing
       whether at live music events
              sitting in small, cozy coffee houses,
       or basking under the silence of the sun.

Be aware of the calling,
       for tomorrow
              the very last apple shall be plucked from the
       family orchard.

Walking Skeleton

Your fate, if fortunate enough to flip through close to a century of
pages,
      will still end up being that of a walking skeleton.

Then, in your obsolete weakness,
      gone is the ability to merge with Porsches, beach walks or
mountain excursions.

      There is little interest in dancing with the living dead.

The reign of an emperor is short
      and ever at risk,
            both from rival regional rulers
but also,
      from time itself.

The Fading Gravestone

Despite lustrous and hard-fought battles for the homeland,
even the most prestigious and decorated of soldiers inherit a
gravestone
that shall fade to nothingness.

This is what the world just does.
To the vagabond, to the gladiator, to the king.

Shine

Don't protect anything for the sake of mere preservation.
      Not just in the wealth sense,
            but also, in the soul sense.
Drape your jewelry.
      Rubies are not meant to be vaulted.
Why give gemstones the same finality as a corpse locked away in
permanent forgottenness?

Tonight, our diamonds and gold shall shine.

An aspect of immortality juxtaposed to a physique
      falling apart towards its morbid fate.

Let Our Eyes Visit and Dance

Let our eyes visit and dance
because the days are discounted.

The early orange sun is spectacular
        but in the radiance,
                sadness for the sensation subsiding.

Today's narration becomes tomorrow's epic tale.

Stories start somewhere.

The same can be said for regret. The same is always said for regret.

You, Deprived of Potential

For most, the business of existence
is often the imitation of everyone
with nothing to show for this copy-cat behavior
except the draining of genuineness and integrity.

The calamity of life is acting out a script
not written by you.

Create on your own terms
before the curtains close.

Bad Contract

Sacrificing some witnessing is understandable.

But giving most of your life away
for the mere potential of a few years of retirement
        a period when the body becomes debilitated
                and travel is ever more futile?

These are very bad contract terms.

We Pass Through

We pass through
      with the false impression that ownership is real.

The land knows us but for only so little
      before attending to other sons and daughters.

Today, the World Trembles

Tomorrow,
at best,
an overlooked statue in some obscure courtyard
may be erected in your honor.

But today,
today,
the world trembles
at what is possible
with your own hands.

Dust and Weeds

The drink is for drinking.
The hills are for hiking.

Tomorrow, there shall be no taste of sweets on your lips,
nor will even a toe be planted on any road.

All you shall do is collect dust and weeds.
and even then,
none of it will be of your own accord.

Ponder Your Prospective Burial Plot

Ponder your prospective burial plot.

Sacrifice but a few hours and nurse the spot
that shall cradle you for eternity.

Let the inevitable be a catalyst for a life of no expectations.

Grim is the prescription.
Grimmer still, the avoidance of fate.

I Always Have Tomorrow

"I always have tomorrow."

What cowardly words
      hiding behind an expectation
            that somehow, this existence shall provide you
another chance.

The audacity to believe that you are owed something,
                      something more than *this*, *now*.

Enjoy the safety that dwells in the delay.

In due course,
      the final leaf flutters in late fall
          and all hope becomes barren.

There is no new spring season to come and save you.

Directions

Loved ones who remain
     debate directions,
        whether to take the back roads
or stay further on the freeway
     wondering which way serves as the closest conduit to
your grave.

Worry not.

     Whether they shave off a few seconds,
        or somehow get lost and arrive late,
your bones will be going nowhere.

This discussion of theirs will ever so quickly vanish into the air
     as they go back to being about their business
while you stay,
forever
     none the wiser.

Tomorrow Plays Dangerous Games

The promises of aspirations
are ever more at risk of sliding into the land of the never
happened.

Tomorrow plays dangerous games.

Upon news of your death,
          mourners speak of your unrealized goals.

Discussions of what you had your sights on to achieve,
          spoken with soft tones
                    with pity and sorrow
knowing that these plans are now eternally impossible.

Witnesses No More

The sun warns us twice:
once in the morning, as if to say, "Count your blessings to see me
again today,"

and the second,

when it gradually falls away.

While its beauty dates back billions of years
our eyes shall eventually become blank,
                                    when we are reduced to
                        nothingness.
Witnesses no more.

Therefore, it is our utmost duty to become drained from
awareness,
            so spent from such serious sight-seeing
that there won't be a minute to ever accept anything outside of
the admiration of all.

An Imam Informs the Village of Your Death

There shall be
at some point
at the 11:00am hour
a death announcement over your village,

by an imam that likely knows you not.

Faint family memories, with a few acquaintances stopping their
daily chores
to process the newly received information.

But the day is young,
and your life is now gone.

The café is far enough, and loud enough,
that a heavy minority may not hear a word,
neither in Albanian, nor Arabic, nor any other language.

A memory is only a memory if registered as one.

Your descendants shall reach travel destinations they so desired,
but their witnessings are not your witnessings,
since you traded in the marvelous for the supposed necessary.

So take heed,
        for the mountain pathways still lie clear,
                and antique leather books
                        are begging to be broken open.

The death announcement never veers from its appointed time.
        Just ensure all actions before this weighted day
                were completely ones of ownership, and ones of
        love.

We Await Your Company

Grave markers directly face the city street,
        with others watching over from a hillside,
saying without saying

"We await your arrival to this everlasting abode."

Time Kills in Different Ways

Time strips buildings
and buries people.

There is no punchline to this poem.

Soon

What, today?

In which state shall we salute the sun?
Upright and attentive, or sleepy and sluggish?

Remember, no one else cares.

Do the gods concern themselves with the opinions of mere
mortals?

Surely not.

Treat yourself as the divinity you are.
Let every decision be decisive in plan and in purpose.

Or, if you so choose,
combust spontaneously.

But drive. Just drive.

Conquer colosseums,
          impart knowledge onto wide-eyed descendants,
                    or get lost in love.

Answer only to the boss of authenticity.

Who you are is only for you to decide.

Soon,

          wild grass shall grow over all that we once
     thought would be us forever.

Until

By embracing the inevitable,
        become satisfied with each dawn and each moonlight
        and all splendor in between.

The night sky shares secrets,
and the morning dew imports wisdom.

Speak gracefully and love eloquently.
In the eventual sits the beautiful.
Each smile, each kiss,
each breath
        elevates the everyday,
                until
well, until.

The Wasted Life

How many times has the sun risen and fallen
and seen you, unaltered, and none the attentive.

This had the sun wondering why your soul sits so statically
stuck in the space of the same?

Day upon day upon day.
Waste upon waste, upon waste.

Never Let the Eventual Steal the Now

Have your celebrations
and do so without any thought for tomorrow.
Never let the eventual
steal the now.

Tomorrow Erases All Evidence

Sing your songs
for tomorrow appears
and erases all evidence of jovial notes.

A fundamentalist
      with neither the interest nor taste for music.

The Only Certainty

The days linger
until an entire life has passed.

In boredom,
the seeds of regret.

Become infatuated with life.

Death does not allow for the possibility
of remedying errors and oversights.

Being alive is the language of all universes.

The Shortness of Life

Listen to what the winds whisper.

Today, they tell you secrets.

But tomorrow

they are off flirting in someone
else's ear.

Tomorrows Cannot Be Banked

Tomorrows cannot be banked for some later date.

What is not used shall eventually disintegrate.

Therefore,
       hold the hours with hands of holiness.

Leave a mark with your living.

We must all walk the plank.
                    Some just do so
liberated.

An Illustrious Past

Infused with the nutrients of the soil,
we embark upon an age of growth.

Push up and out into the world.

Radiate.

And when the withering commences
reflect back
on an illustrious past.

The Elixir for Living Forever

Take so seriously the way you stir your spoon.

See everything with magnificent marvel
with purity
with precision, and with utter intensity.

Pain may have a propensity to swallow everything whole
        but it is powerless against the ones
                who dwell in deceptively simple circumstances
outside yesterday
outside tomorrow
outside time.

Engulfed in prominent presence.

The elixir for living forever.

The Voice of a Life Ignored

Why, child
did tuck away your ambitions
far into the bottom of some storage chest?

The heart forgets not
      knowing quite well
            (and often reminded in the dead of night)
that those desires still struggle to speak.

I recommend its best for you to cover your ears
      and pray for empty dreams,
because
      nothing sounds worse
         and is harder to dismiss
            than the voice of a life ignored.

No Hold on the *Now*

Become disinterested in anything that isn't your everything.

Curse away whatever falls outside the bounds of necessity
        and live
here,
right here.

Time is on a warpath of destruction.

But become utterly indifferent.
        Stand tall
        and stare that devil straight in the eyes
and smile,
        since you understand
that this beast has
                no hold on the *now*.

Few

The days left drinking coffee,
tasting Belgian chocolate,
or laughing deeply with the children
        are few.

The fresh dew
and the sounds of geese over grayed skies
are too,
        so few.

Smile.

Smile radically at anything and everyone.

Be content by being content.

Love without apology
        and
die without thought.

The unfoldings are sacred,
        but again,
        few.

When Death Decides That Enough is Enough

Warm winter mornings
sheltered from frost bitten conditions which permeate just
                                                    outside the
                                    circle of safety.

The line between life and death is razor thin.

Use the advantages given and
illuminate absolute authenticity.

For tomorrow
the walls that now guard you become powerless,
when death decides

that enough is enough.

The Janitor

The dance floor is spacious
        with more than enough room
for you to lose yourself.

Be wild in your movement
        and let the onlookers judge.

Know that these voices will often be the loudest
on the day you depart.

Leave footprints
without the slightest regard for any scuffing of surface.

The janitor will eventually arrive
and wash away everything anyway.

Golden Apples

Taste the *now*
and do so religiously,
while offering neither excuses nor apologies.

The golden apples are always tempting,
and their promise, eternal.

But they are forever outside of our taste,
and always returned to the Garden of the Hesperides.

The Intruder

Somewhere,
       some plot of land
sits still
       unassuming in nature
              unaware that at some point
the earth will be disrupted
       torn apart
              inconvenienced with bulldozers and shovels
a breaking of ground
       to make room for an
       intruder
              who will forever occupy a territory
                    that no emperor ever dared dream to
       conquer.

They Curse the Grounds That Encapsulate Their No Longer

Why weep at gravesites?

Understandably, we miss the deceased
        and our tears serve as some sign of respect.

But if those gone were to see you approaching the cemetery,
        certainly
you would hear them shout with anger
        yelling for you to turn around immediately
                to sprint away from this country of the gone,
to return to life,
to return to living.

They curse the grounds that encapsulate their no longer.

Walk and Witness

Don't dare take for granted nature and its sustenance to the soul.

Why rot away indoors?

Our fate lies in sturdy casket walls.

Now,
            and only *now,*
                        is the time to walk and witness.

There is No Better Day

The percentage of people
who secretly house a "hopefully" in their hearts
is staggeringly high.

The masses deceive themselves
                by staking everything on the seeds of some
dream that they pray will come to fruition.
Yet not a drop of water has graced said dormant seeds.

The farmer who fails to toil shall have no success growing what
sits isolated and uncared for.

The hours pass quickly,
        with time taking everything.

But here,
        most just give up what matters willfully.

There is no better day than today to tend to your garden.

Not tomorrow
Not next week
Not in some other life that will never arrive.

Nothing Spared

Tomorrow can only be recycled so many times.

The boulevard eventually becomes barren.

Cities that stood prestigious
are now buried well into the ground, well into the past, well into
the lost.

Understand that even the most mighty have met this silent
demise.

There will eventually be no trace of being whatsoever.

No horns,
No sirens,

nothing.

What is most shocking of all
is the level of delusion--
                people who go about
thinking that somehow
they shall be the sole survivors.

Quit Harboring Hostilities

Quit harboring hostilities
at what is yet to unfold
      and that that may never take form.

Every moment in regret
is a lost opportunity to shine the singular sacred.

The now of now is now.

And tomorrow,
      neither trace of sorrows, successes, or subjective
expectations
of what was supposedly meant to be.

The World is Today Forever Yours

Background colors
heavily coated with permanent paint.

Witness the inevitable with open palms
empty pockets
and the special concession
that tomorrow
someone else will be the one to receive the bounty of awareness,
        leaving you
an afterthought in the realization of existence,
        included in the history of those rarely in love with living.

The world is today forever yours.

There are No Alms for the Deceased

Not one person will
    visit your grave
        and offer a second of their time for you to eat,
            let alone breath.
There are no alms for the deceased.

Remember that on this day
    when these monsters
        scheme to steal what is sacred.

These Roads Will Forget Your Name

"This branch is now closed."

A sign used for business,
        but may as well be applied
                to anyone that grew up
                        in the city they call
                        home.

These roads will
        at some point
                forget your name.
The golden child no more.

And Just Like That...

And just like that
the heart strikes intensely,
lastly.
An undoubtedly permanent non-pulsation.

Ultimately,
what is there to show for the man who
delayed devouring life with the defiant
determination so needed to stake claim
to conquering this condition called
existence?

A few fleeting flashes of exhilaration,
outweighed handedly by tens of thousands of suppressed
visions of fulfilment,
all ending with a frantic family,
a few police cars,
an ambulance,
and some nosy
neighbors.

A depressing departure activated.

A cold, cold send off
for someone too afraid to wander out into the unknown,
unwilling to die in the field of freedom.

An obituary that can be written with a billion different fonts,
using (more or less) the same words,
capturing the same message of squandered
opportunities.

Ethereal encounters that could have elevated us from animals to
the heights of divinity.

Death Knows No Peace Treaty

Sleep through nothing.

The morning comes to check in and ensure the eyes
       are ready for love.

Death knows neither cease fire
       nor armistice,
       nor truce,
       nor treaty.

The battlegrounds for life are clear.

Dancing With Rain

Measure the raindrops
not by the speed of which
one hustles from the car to the coffee shop.

      But rather
by not counting at all.

The same rain will more than sufficiently soak
      the top of your tomb.

So, for as long you can,
      make this a two-way dance.

Orban's Canon

Be cognizant of the time yet spent.
The fortress of youth is always attacked by all sides.

Orban's canon is sure to breech the walls.
      The empire will fast fall.

There are few to say extensive eulogies at your wake.
A moment of remembrance
      and then off to conquer new lands.

A few lines in a few history books.
      That is all that shall remain.

New rulers crown themselves kings,
oblivious to the fact that they will find themselves
      succumbed to the same forceful fate.

Knockout

Death does the most damage
when it delivers a one-two punch.

It likes to show its challengers
that the initial jab
which pales in comparison to a secondary kill shot.

Onlookers
who hold their beloved in the highest regard
are left silent
            powerless
and lost in their grief of what they just observed in the ring.

This is how our lives will play out.

Death deems desires worthless in its calculation and gameplan of
who goes next.

Wait not for the fatal blow
but flutter around the ring smiling.

For Something That Means Nothing

Death can only be destroyed
by drowning the murderer in indifference.

I have killed you by neither knowing
        nor not knowing
        your existence.

The sun speaks to me so fully with rays
and the flowers flood my senses
with both sight and smell
that I have no time
        nor use
              for something that means nothing.

Today is the Registration of Your Sacredness

The ground,
        it comes to envelop all of us.
Suffocating in strength
        undefeated in destroying the formerly vibrant.

Make sure your steps are serious, yet playful
and incalculable in unpredictably.

Whatever you so choose
        choose that.

That which is beneath you
is beneath you.

Today is the registration of your sacredness.
Free,
unwavering,
pure.

Ask Your Perished Self

The clear vision that this all ends tomorrow
      should be more than enough
            to rebel in the rowdiest of ways.

Ask the person with a walking disability
      what they would give for healthy legs.
Ask the blind for the price of witnessing eyes.
Ask your perished self
      the value of even one extra day.

The cost never outweighs the asymmetrical return.

Just Not Yet

How many days of full living are there?

De-rack the bespoke suit and wear it with elation.
Today, the body dons the cloth of a prince.

Why call your best suit your "funeral" suit?
Wearing it in death provides not the slightest satisfaction.

The thrill of fashion will then be irrelevant,
as is the excitement of anything else, really.

Therefore, stroll through the city not to flaunt
            but to be reminded
that death

            is your future too.

Just not yet.

Inscriptions of Prospects

A beautiful morning.

Cautious clouds
revealing just a peek of the sun.

Fresh dew is the evidence of awakening.
A new turning of the page.
A new lease on life.

The end is the end is the end.

Violens play somberly
            while the casket is lowered into nothingness,
                  and the farewell is anything but well.
All before carried inscriptions of prospects,
            what now are faded, forgotten, forsaken.

Nothing

Nothing will remain.

Nothing.

Not your words,
Not your worries,
Not your naysayers.

Nothing.

Don't Be Memory Poor

Spend,
  spend at least some of it.

The future has you by the arm,
  dictating decisions that might leave you dollar rich
    but memory poor.

I am not saying to not save.

But having piles of money is insignificant

compared to the void of not attending an event that you and your children will savor
  decades past the day of experience.

Fresh, Full Days

Breathe, oh living one.

Breathe in oxygen deeply.
      A religious experience with every inhale and exhale.

The satisfaction is but a temporary one
        for in due time,
there will be no witnessing
        no encounter
              no divine interaction
                    of and with
these fresh, full days.